TAPAS

Spanish Appetizers

KÖNEMANN

Tapas

Tapas are at the heart of Spanish life. A delicious portion of fresh seafood, cured olives or spicy chorizo with a chilled glass of sherry can be enjoyed in cafés and taverns all over Spain.

The word tapas comes from *tapa*, meaning 'to cover'. At first this is exactly what tapas were—a slice of bread or ham placed on top of a glass of sherry in a bar or tavern to keep off the flies. These salty complimentary morsels also promoted thirst, and hopefully extra drink sales!

Tapas have evolved since then and are now often the main reason for visiting a tavern. Tapas today represent more than just good food; they are a whole way of life in Spain. Spaniards don't usually eat lunch until around 2 or 3 pm, and dinner until around 10 at night, so tapas are eaten with a cold drink, among good friends, to stave off the hunger pangs created by eating so late. (Though whether tapas were created to fit this gap, or dinner hours just became later to allow time for tapas, remains a mystery.)

Tapas don't always fit the mold of appetizers. Though they are sold in small portions, many of the dishes seem more like a first or even main course, and can be as imaginative as the chef.

The taste of Spanish food is not as hot and spicy as the cooking of South America, though it has borrowed many of the same ingredients. It uses the best produce, simply prepared, from

From left to right: caper berries; cheese; chorizo; shrimp with lemon wedges; prosciutto; pickled onions; Marinated red sweet peppers (page 59); Marinated olives (pages 20–21); Banana chiles with garlic (page 22) and Artichokes in aromatic vinaigrette (page 26)

fresh seafood, sun-ripened tomatoes and sweet peppers, to regional dishes made with smoked meats and fish, often flavored with saffron, paprika and rich olive oil.

You don't need to follow any special rules when serving tapas. They are perfect finger food for a drinks party, can be served as appetizers for a small dinner party, or can even replace the whole meal for a large gathering.

The recipes in this book serve about four people if eaten with a number of other dishes. If you want the tapas to replace a full meal, allow about two recipes per head, and provide plenty of crusty bread to soak up the delicious juices and sauces. Good-quality Spanish extra virgin olive oil is a good purchase and will add lots of flavor to dishes (though you need only ordinary olive oil for frying).

Small earthenware dishes give an authentic touch and are useful for serving as the tapas can often be both cooked and served in them.

Many tapas are eaten cold or at room temperature and can be served buffet style. Other tapas can be made ahead of time, but need finishing off at the last minute. Place in a dish and pass round while piping hot.

What to drink? Soft drinks, beer, wine or a jug of icy sangria all complement tapas, but for a real Spanish experience, nothing beats chilled dry sherry.

Tapas

If you're having a tapas party, pick a mixture of hot and cold dishes, and choose some recipes that can be prepared in advance so that you have time to enjoy yourself on the day.

❖ ❖ ❖

Ham and olive empanadillas

Preparation time:
  45 minutes +
  5 minutes cooling
Total cooking time:
  25 minutes
Makes about 15

2 eggs
1/4 cup stuffed green
  olives, chopped
2/3 cup finely chopped
  cooked ham
1/4 cup shredded
  Cheddar
3 sheets ready-rolled
  puff pastry, thawed
1 egg yolk, lightly
  beaten

1. Place the eggs in a small saucepan, cover with water and bring to a boil. Boil for 10 minutes, then drain and cool for 5 minutes in cold water. Peel and chop.
2. Combine the eggs, green olives, ham and Cheddar in a large bowl. Preheat the oven to 425°F. Lightly grease two baking sheets.
3. Cut the puff pastry sheets into 4 inch rounds. (You should be able to cut about five rounds from each sheet.) Spoon a tablespoon of the ham and olive mixture into the center of each round, fold the pastry over to encase the filling and crimp the edges firmly to seal.
4. Place the pastries on the baking sheets, about 3/4 inch apart. Brush with the egg yolk and bake in the center to top half of the oven for 15 minutes, or until well browned and puffed. Switch the baking sheets around after 10 minutes and cover loosely with foil if the empanadillas start to become too brown. Serve hot.

NUTRITION PER EMPANADILLA
*Protein 5 g; Fat 10 g;
Carbohydrate 12 g; Dietary
Fiber 1 g; Cholesterol
50 mg; 160 calories*

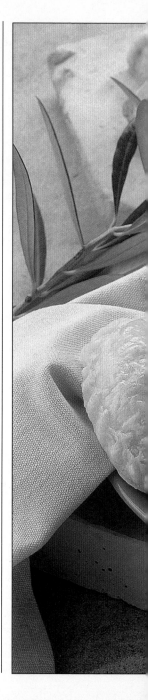

Ham and olive empanadillas

Veal sausages in white wine

Preparation time:
  10 minutes
Total cooking time:
  10 minutes
Serves 4

2 teaspoons olive oil
4 thin veal sausages
  (see Note)
1 clove garlic,
  chopped
1/2 cup dry white
  wine
1/4 cup chicken
  stock
2 teaspoons chopped
  fresh flat-leaf parsley

1. Heat the oil in a skillet over medium heat, add the sausages and cook for 5 minutes, turning to brown all over. Drain on paper towels. Cool slightly and cut diagonally into 1 1/4 inch pieces.
2. Add the garlic to the hot pan and cook, stirring, over medium heat for 30 seconds. Increase the heat to high and add the wine and chicken stock. Simmer for 3 minutes, or until the liquid is reduced by about two-thirds (there should be just a little liquid left in the pan). Return the sausages to the pan and stir for 30 seconds to reheat. Remove from the heat, stir in the parsley and season with salt and freshly ground black pepper. Serve hot with crusty bread.

NUTRITION PER SERVE
Protein 11 g; Fat 3 g; Carbohydrate 0.5 g; Dietary Fiber 0 g; Cholesterol 40 mg; 98 calories

Note: Veal sausages are available from good butchers and specialty markets, and are often made with pork and veal. Italian sweet sausages are also a good choice.

Spanish-style beef kebabs

Preparation time:
  15 minutes + 2 hours
  marinating
Total cooking time:
  5 minutes
Makes 12

12 x 6 inch wooden
  skewers
2 lb round steak
3 cloves garlic,
  chopped
1 tablespoon chopped
  fresh flat-leaf parsley
1/3 cup lemon juice
1/2 teaspoon black
  pepper

Paprika dressing
2 teaspoons paprika
large pinch cayenne
  pepper
1/2 teaspoon salt
2 tablespoons red wine
  vinegar
1/3 cup olive oil

1. Soak the skewers in water for 1 hour, or until they sink, to make sure that they don't burn during cooking.
2. Trim the excess fat from the steak and cut into 1 1/4 inch pieces. Combine the steak, garlic, parsley, lemon juice and pepper in a nonreactive bowl, cover with plastic wrap and marinate for 2 hours in the refrigerator.
3. To make the paprika dressing, whisk the paprika, cayenne pepper, salt, vinegar and oil together until well blended.
4. Preheat a lightly oiled barbecue grill or broiler pan. Thread the pieces of marinated meat onto the skewers, then cook the kebabs, turning once, for about 5–6 minutes, or until cooked through. Drizzle with the paprika dressing and serve hot with wedges of lemon or a mixed lettuce salad.

NUTRITION PER KEBAB
Protein 20 g; Fat 8.5 g; Carbohydrate 0.5 g; Dietary Fiber 0 g; Cholesterol 55 mg; 160 calories

Veal sausages in white wine (top) with Spanish-style beef kebabs

Calamari à la Romana

Preparation time:
10 minutes +
30 minutes
refrigeration
Total cooking time:
10 minutes
Serves 4

12 oz cleaned small
 squid hoods
1/2 teaspoon salt
1/3 cup all-purpose
 flour
1/4 teaspoon black
 pepper
oil, for deep-frying
lemon wedges,
 to serve

1. Cut the squid into
1/2 inch wide rings.
Combine the squid
rings with the salt,
cover and refrigerate
for 30 minutes, then
dry on paper towels.
2. Combine the flour
and pepper in a bowl.
Fill a deep, heavy-based
saucepan a third full of
oil and heat to 350°F (a
cube of bread dropped
in the oil will brown in
15 seconds). Flour a
few squid rings and
deep-fry, turning with a
long-handled spoon, for
3 minutes, or until
lightly browned and
crisp. Flour the
remaining batches just
before frying. Drain on
crumpled paper towels

and serve hot with the
lemon wedges.

NUTRITION PER SERVE
*Protein 15 g; Fat 3.5 g;
Carbohydrate 7 g; Dietary
Fiber 0.5 g; Cholesterol
175 mg; 125 calories*

Patatas bravas

Preparation time:
15 minutes
Total cooking time:
55 minutes
Serves 6

1 lb 8 oz all-purpose
 potatoes, cut into
 1 1/2 inch pieces
1/4 cup olive oil

Spicy tomato sauce
1 tablespoon olive
 oil
1 small onion,
 chopped
1 clove garlic,
 crushed
1/2 teaspoon ground
 cumin
1/2 teaspoon dried chili
 flakes
1 teaspoon paprika
1/4 cup dry white
 wine
2 ripe tomatoes, finely
 chopped
1 tablespoon tomato
 paste
dash Tabasco sauce
1 tablespoon coarsely
 chopped fresh
 flat-leaf parsley

1. Preheat the oven to
425°F. Place the potato
pieces in a 12 x 8 inch
baking dish, pour the
oil over, sprinkle with
some salt and toss to
coat. Bake in the top
half of the oven for
40 minutes, turning
once, until the potatoes
are cooked through and
light brown.
2. To make the spicy
tomato sauce, heat the
oil in a saucepan over
medium heat, add the
onion and cook,
stirring occasionally,
for 3 minutes. Add the
garlic, cumin, chili and
paprika and cook for
1 minute. Increase the
heat to high, add the
wine and simmer for
30 seconds, then reduce
the heat to medium and
add the tomatoes and
tomato paste. Cook,
stirring occasionally,
for 10 minutes, or until
the mixture is thick.
3. Process the sauce
in a food processor
or blender until
smooth. Return the
sauce to the saucepan
to reheat and stir in the
Tabasco, parsley and
some salt. Pour the
sauce over the potatoes
and serve hot.

NUTRITION PER SERVE
*Protein 4.5 g; Fat 15 g;
Carbohydrate 20 g; Dietary
Fiber 3.5 g; Cholesterol
0 mg; 220 calories*

*Calamari à la Romana (top) with
Patatas bravas*

Scallop seviche

Preparation time:
  20 minutes +
  2 hours marinating
Total cooking time:
  None
Makes 15

*15 scallops on the half
  shell (with roe,
  optional)
1 teaspoon finely
  grated lime rind
2 cloves garlic, chopped
2 fresh red chiles,
  seeded and chopped
1/4 cup lime juice
1 tablespoon chopped
  fresh parsley
1 tablespoon olive oil*

1. Take the scallops
off their half shell. If
the scallops need to be
cut off the shell, use a
small, sharp paring
knife to carefully slice
the attached part away
from the shell, being
careful to leave as little
scallop meat on the
shell as possible.
Remove the dark vein
and white muscle, and
wash the shells.
2. In a nonreactive
bowl, mix together the
lime rind, garlic, chiles,
lime juice, parsley and
olive oil and season
with salt and freshly
ground black pepper.
Place the scallops in the
dressing and stir to
coat. Cover with plastic
wrap and marinate in
the refrigerator for
2 hours to 'cook' the
scallop meat.
3. To serve, slide the
scallops back onto
a half shell and spoon
the dressing over.
Serve cold.

NUTRITION PER SCALLOP
*Protein 1.5 g; Fat 1.5 g;
Carbohydrate 0.5 g; Dietary
Fiber 0 g; Cholesterol
4 mg; 20 calories*

Note: These scallops
will keep for up to
2 days in the dressing.

Borek of asparagus

Preparation time:
  20 minutes
Total cooking time:
  25 minutes
Makes 16

*16 fresh asparagus
  spears
1/2 teaspoon salt
1/2 teaspoon black
  pepper
2 tablespoons grated
  lemon rind
2 sheets ready-rolled
  puff pastry, thawed
1 egg yolk
1 tablespoon sesame
  seeds*

1. Preheat the oven
to 400°F.
2. Add the asparagus
to a large skillet of
lightly salted boiling
water and simmer for
about 3 minutes, then
drain and refresh under
cold running water.
Trim to 4 inch lengths.
3. Combine the salt,
black pepper and
lemon rind in a shallow
dish and roll each
asparagus spear lightly
in this mixture.
4. Cut the puff pastry
sheets into 5 x 2 1/2 inch
rectangles and place
one asparagus spear on
each piece of pastry.
In a bowl, combine
the egg yolk with
2 teaspoons water and
brush on the sides and
ends of the pastry. Roll
the pastry up like a
package, folding in the
sides so that the
asparagus is completely
sealed in. Press the
seams of the pastry
using a fork.
5. Place the pastries on
lightly greased baking
sheets. Brush with the
remaining egg and
sprinkle lightly with the
sesame seeds.
6. Bake the asparagus
pastries for about
15–20 minutes, or
until golden brown.
These pastries are
delicious served
warm or cold.

NUTRITION PER PASTRY
*Protein 2 g; Fat 6 g;
Carbohydrate 7.5 g; Dietary
Fiber 0.5 g; Cholesterol
30 mg; 95 calories*

---

*Scallop seviche (top) with
Borek of asparagus*

White garlic soup with grapes

Preparation time:
  20 minutes + 1 hour
  refrigeration
Total cooking time:
  None
Serves 4

1 cup soft white bread
  crumbs
3/4 cup milk
3/4 cup blanched
  almonds
2 cloves garlic, coarsely
  chopped
2 tablespoons extra
  virgin olive oil
2 tablespoons sherry
  vinegar
1 1/2 cups iced
  water
3/4 cup seedless green
  grapes, peeled

1. Place the bread
crumbs in a small bowl,
add the milk and allow
to soak for 5 minutes.
2. Put the almonds,
garlic and some salt in a
food processor and
process until fine (do
not overprocess as the
almonds may become
oily). Add the soaked
bread crumbs and
process until just
smooth, then add the
olive oil gradually and
process until the
mixture is thick
and creamy.
3. Transfer to a large
bowl and gradually stir

in the vinegar and
water. Cover and place
in the refrigerator for
1 hour until chilled
thoroughly. Season with
salt and serve with the
grapes floating on top.

NUTRITION PER SERVE
*Protein 10 g; Fat 30 g;
Carbohydrate 20 g; Dietary
Fiber 4 g; Cholesterol
6 mg; 395 calories*

Bean salad

Preparation time:
  15 minutes +
  overnight soaking +
  1 hour marinating
Total cooking time:
  55 minutes
Serves 4–6

1 cup dried lima beans
  (see Note)
2 eggs
1/2 cup stuffed green
  olives, sliced
1 clove garlic, finely
  chopped
1 tablespoon chopped
  fresh flat-leaf parsley
2 tablespoons extra
  virgin olive oil
1 tablespoon red wine
  vinegar
1/4 teaspoon paprika

1. Soak the beans in
plenty of water
overnight. Drain. Add
the beans to a saucepan
of boiling water, return

to the boil and cook,
partially covered, over
medium heat for
35–45 minutes, or until
tender but not mushy
(some beans may take
longer). Drain.
2. Place the eggs in a
small saucepan, cover
with water and bring
to a boil. Boil for
10 minutes, then drain
and cool for 5 minutes
in cold water. Peel
and chop.
3. Combine the beans,
eggs, olives, garlic
and parsley in a bowl.
Whisk together the
olive oil, vinegar,
paprika and some salt
and freshly ground
black pepper until
well blended. Pour over
the bean mixture and
mix well to coat with
the dressing.
4. Cover the salad
and let stand for at
least 1 hour at room
temperature to
marinate before serving.
The salad can also be
refrigerated overnight;
the longer it is left, the
stronger the garlic
flavor will be.

NUTRITION PER SERVE (6)
*Protein 4.5 g; Fat 8.5 g;
Carbohydrate 4 g; Dietary
Fiber 2.5 g; Cholesterol
60 mg; 110 calories*

Note: Chickpeas could
be used instead of lima
beans in this recipe.

---

*White garlic soup with grapes (top) and
Bean salad*

Spread the tahini paste over the pastry sheets, all the way to the edges.

Fold the pastry sheet from each side so that it meets in the middle.

Tahini and chili palmiers

Preparation time:
  25 minutes +
  30 minutes refrigeration
Total cooking time:
  20 minutes
Makes 32

1/2 cup tahini (sesame
  seed) paste
1 fresh red chile, seeded
  and finely chopped
1/2 teaspoon paprika
2 sheets ready-rolled
  puff pastry, thawed

1. Preheat the oven
to 400°F.
2. Combine the tahini
paste, chile and paprika
in a bowl and season
with some salt. Spread
this paste over both
puff pastry sheets,
making sure that the
paste goes all the way
to the edges.

3. Take one pastry sheet
and fold from opposite
sides until the folds
meet in the middle.
Then fold one side over
the other to resemble a
closed book. Repeat
with the remaining
pastry sheet and tahini
mixture. Refrigerate
the pastry at this stage
for at least 30 minutes
to firm it up and make
it easier to work with.
4. Cut the pastry into
1/2 inch slices. Cover
two baking sheets with
parchment paper and
place the palmiers on
them, making sure that
the palmiers are not too
close to one another
because they will spread
during cooking.
5. Bake the palmiers for
10–12 minutes on one
side, then flip them over
and bake for another
5–6 minutes, or until
golden and cooked
through. They are
delicious served at

room temperature
or cold.

NUTRITION PER PALMIER
*Protein 1.5 g; Fat 5 g;
Carbohydrate 4 g; Dietary
Fiber 1 g; Cholesterol
2.5 mg; 65 calories*

Note: To freeze the
palmiers, place the
sliced, uncooked
palmiers on a baking
sheet and freeze until
firm, then seal in plastic
bags. When ready to
cook, place the frozen
palmiers on the two
paper-lined baking
sheets and allow to
thaw, then cook
following the steps
above. The cooked
palmiers can be stored
in an airtight container
for up to 1 week. If the
palmiers soften, recrisp
in a 350°F oven for
3–5 minutes, then cool
on a wire rack.
For an alternative
filling, spread the
pastry thinly with some
tapenade or sun-dried
tomato paste.

Tahini and chili palmiers

*Fold one side over the other to resemble a
closed book.*

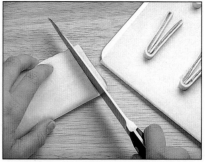

*Cut the pastry into 1/2 inch slices with a
sharp knife.*

Stuffed sweet peppers

Preparation time:
  40 minutes + cooling
Total cooking time:
  20 minutes
Makes about 20

5 large red sweet bell
  peppers
1/4 cup butter
1 small boiling onion,
  finely chopped
1 clove garlic, crushed
1/4 cup all-purpose
  flour
1 cup milk
3 x 3 1/2 oz cans tuna in
  oil, drained
1 tablespoon chopped
  fresh flat-leaf parsley
2/3 cup flour, extra
2 eggs, lightly beaten
1/2 teaspoon paprika
2/3 cup dry bread
  crumbs
oil, for deep-frying

1. Preheat the broiler.
Cut the peppers into
quarters. Broil, skin-
side-up, until the skin
blackens and blisters.
Place in a plastic bag
and let cool, then peel.
2. Heat the butter in a
saucepan over medium
heat. Add the onion
and cook, stirring, for
2 minutes, or until soft.
Add the garlic and cook
for 1 minute. Add the
1/4 cup flour and stir
for 1 minute, or until
bubbly and just

beginning to change
color. Remove from the
heat and gradually pour
in the milk, stirring
until smooth. Return
to the heat and stir for
1 minute, or until the
mixture boils and
thickens and leaves the
side of the pan. Stir in
the tuna, parsley and
some salt. Transfer to a
bowl, cover with plastic
wrap and allow to cool.
3. Spoon 1 tablespoon
of the filling onto the
bottom end of each
pepper quarter, roll up
and secure with a
cocktail pick. Place the
extra flour in a dish,
the eggs in a shallow
bowl and combine the
paprika and crumbs in
another shallow dish.
4. Coat the peppers in
the flour, then the eggs,
allowing the excess to
drip away, then toss in
the crumbs.
5. Fill a deep, heavy-
based saucepan a third
full of oil and heat to
350°F (a cube of bread
dropped in the oil will
brown in 15 seconds).
Deep-fry in batches for
2 minutes, or until
golden. Drain on paper
towels and remove the
picks. Serve hot.

NUTRITION PER CAPSICUM
*Protein 6 g; Fat 7.5 g;
Carbohydrate 5 g; Dietary
Fiber 0.5 g; Cholesterol
35 mg; 110 calories*

Braised fennel

Preparation time:
  15 minutes
Total cooking time:
  20 minutes
Serves 4

1 fresh fennel bulb
1/2 onion, cut into thin
  wedges
1/2 teaspoon sugar
2 tablespoons lemon
  juice
1/3 cup olive oil

1. Preheat the oven to
350°F. Trim the outer
layers off the fennel
and cut in half through
the core. Cut each half
into eight wedges,
being careful to cut
each piece through
the core so that it
stays intact.
2. Lay the fennel and
onion in a baking dish
and sprinkle with the
sugar. Pour the lemon
juice, olive oil and
2 tablespoons water
over, then season with
salt and pepper. Cover
with parchment paper,
then foil, and bake for
20 minutes, or until the
fennel is soft but not
falling apart. Serve hot.

NUTRITION PER SERVE
*Protein 1.5 g; Fat 20 g;
Carbohydrate 5.5 g; Dietary
Fiber 4 g; Cholesterol
0 mg; 200 calories*

*Stuffed sweet peppers (top) with
Braised fennel*

Broiled sardines with cucumber

Preparation time:
  20 minutes +
  30 minutes marinating
  + 15 minutes draining
Total cooking time:
  10 minutes
Makes 30

30 butterflied sardines,
  without heads
  (see Note)
2 tablespoons olive oil
2 tablespoons vegetable
  oil
2 tablespoons lemon
  juice
2 cloves garlic, sliced
1 tablespoon fresh
  oregano leaves
1 short, thin cucumber
1/4 teaspoon sugar

1. Place half the sardines in a single layer in a nonreactive dish. Combine the olive and vegetable oils, lemon juice, garlic and oregano leaves and pour half over the sardines. Top with the remaining sardines and pour the rest of the oil mixture over. Cover with plastic wrap and marinate for 30 minutes in the refrigerator.
2. Meanwhile, using a wide vegetable peeler, peel strips lengthwise

off the cucumber, making four even sides and avoiding peeling off any cucumber with seeds. You should get 15 slices of cucumber. Cut in half to get 30 slices the same length as the sardines.
3. Lay the cucumber strips flat around the sides and base of a colander and sprinkle with sugar and a little salt. Place over a bowl. Let stand for 15 minutes to drain off any juices.
4. Preheat the broiler. Wash the cucumber well and dry with paper towels. Place a slice of cucumber on the flesh side of each sardine and roll up. Secure with cocktail picks.
5. Place half the sardines under the broiler and cook for 5 minutes, or until cooked through. Repeat with the remaining sardines. Serve warm, perhaps with a bowl of tzatziki.

NUTRITION PER SARDINE
Protein 5 g; Fat 5 g; Carbohydrate 0 g; Dietary Fiber 0 g; Cholesterol 25 mg; 65 calories

Note: Butterflied sardines are sardines that have been gutted, boned and opened out flat.

Carrots and olives

Preparation time:
  25 minutes
Total cooking time:
  15 minutes
Serves 4

2 tablespoons extra
  virgin olive oil
1 lb young carrots,
  cut into 2 x 1/4 inch
  sticks
1 clove garlic, finely
  chopped
1 tablespoon chopped
  fresh flat-leaf parsley
12 Spanish green
  olives, pitted and
  sliced
1 tablespoon slivered
  almonds, lightly
  toasted

1. Heat the olive oil in a heavy-based skillet, add the carrot sticks and cook, covered, over low heat for about 10 minutes, shaking the pan occasionally, until almost tender.
2. Add the garlic, parsley and green olives and stir to combine.
3. Season with salt and freshly ground black pepper, then toss the carrots over low heat for 1 minute. Stir in the slivered almonds and serve warm.

NUTRITION PER SERVE
Protein 2.5 g; Fat 15 g; Carbohydrate 7 g; Dietary Fiber 5 g; Cholesterol 0 mg; 150 calories

Broiled sardines with cucumber (top) and Carrots and olives

Marinated Olives

With their delicious sharp taste, olives are the perfect accompaniment to drinks. Marinating your own olives is easy, and if you make a large batch, they will keep in the refrigerator for months.

TIPS FOR MARINATING

Before marinating the olives, rinse to remove excess saltiness and pat dry with paper towels. Firm olives can then be cracked or scored to help them absorb flavor. To score olives, make two or three cuts down their length. To crack them, do the same, then press firmly between paper towels to flatten them.

Olives should be eaten at room temperature to fully appreciate their flavor, so remove from the refrigerator half an hour before serving. Marinated olives keep for months in sterilized jars if they are totally immersed in olive oil and stored in the refrigerator.

Any extra marinade from the olives can be used as a salad dressing.

LEMON OLIVES WITH VERMOUTH

Mix together 1/4 cup dry vermouth, 1 tablespoon lemon juice, 2 teaspoons shredded lemon rind and 2 tablespoons extra virgin olive oil. Rinse 1 cup Spanish green or stuffed olives and pat dry. Add to the marinade and toss well. Cover and let stand for 1–2 hours or refrigerate overnight.

SPICY WARM OLIVES

Put 1/4 cup extra virgin olive oil, 1 slivered clove garlic, 2 teaspoons chopped fresh thyme, 1 teaspoon chopped fresh rosemary, 1/2 teaspoon each ground cumin and finely chopped fresh red chile and some black pepper in a saucepan.

Rinse 1 cup mixed Spanish black and green olives and pat dry. Add to the pan and heat very gently until the olives are warm and fragrant. Serve immediately.

FRIED OLIVES

Rinse 3/4 cup Spanish green stuffed olives and pat dry. Beat 1 egg lightly in a shallow bowl. Place 1 cup dry bread crumbs in another shallow bowl. Dip the olives one-by-one into the egg, toss in the bread crumbs, then repeat to double crumb the olives. Deep- or pan-fry in light olive oil until golden brown. Drain on paper towels and serve warm. (Do not eat while hot.)

SUN-DRIED TOMATO OLIVES

Rinse 3 cups Spanish black olives and pat dry. Score or crack the olives. Layer in a bowl or jar with 2/3 cup drained and chopped sun-dried tomatoes (reserve the oil), 2 crushed cloves garlic, 2 bay leaves, 1 tablespoon fresh thyme leaves and 2 teaspoons red wine vinegar. Pour in the reserved sun-dried tomato oil and 1 cup extra virgin olive oil, or enough to cover. Cover and let stand for 1–2 hours or refrigerate overnight.

From left to right: Lemon olives with vermouth; Spicy warm olives; Fried olives; Sun-dried tomato olives; Herbed olives

HERBED OLIVES

Mix together 1/4 cup extra virgin olive oil, 1 clove crushed garlic, 2 teaspoons sherry wine vinegar, 1 tablespoon each chopped fresh marjoram and basil, 1 crumbled bay leaf and some black pepper. Rinse 1/2 cup each Spanish black and green olives and pat dry. Add to the marinade and toss well. Cover and let stand for 1–2 hours or refrigerate overnight.

Gambas al pil pil

Preparation time:
  30 minutes +
  30 minutes refrigeration
Total cooking time:
  10 minutes
Serves 4–6

2 lb raw medium
  shrimp
1/2 teaspoon salt
3 tablespoons butter
1/3 cup olive oil
3 cloves garlic, coarsely
  chopped
1/4 teaspoon dried chili
  flakes
1/2 teaspoon paprika

1. Shell and devein the shrimp, keeping the tails intact. Mix the shrimp with the salt in a large bowl, cover and refrigerate for about 30 minutes.
2. Heat the butter and oil together in a flameproof dish over medium heat. When foaming, add the garlic and chili and cook, stirring, for 1 minute, or until golden. Add the shrimp and cook for 3–6 minutes, or until they curl up and change color. Sprinkle with the paprika and serve sizzling hot with plenty of bread for dipping.

NUTRITION PER SERVE (6)
*Protein 35 g; Fat 20 g;
Carbohydrate 0 g; Dietary
Fiber 0 g; Cholesterol
270 mg; 320 calories*

Note: Traditionally, Gambas al pil pil is made and served in small earthenware dishes, with one small dish serving two people. You can make this recipe in two small dishes, just remember that it will cook more quickly.

Banana chiles with garlic

Preparation time:
  10 minutes +
  30 minutes cooling +
  2 days marinating
Total cooking time:
  10 minutes
Serves 6

olive oil, for pan-
  frying
3 cloves garlic
6 banana (Hungarian
  wax) chiles, any
  color
1/4 teaspoon salt
1/4 teaspoon dried
  chili flakes
2 bay leaves
1/2 cup red wine
  vinegar
1/3 cup (80 ml) extra
  virgin olive oil

1. Heat the olive oil in a large skillet over medium heat and add the garlic and banana chiles. Cook for 3 minutes, then place the garlic in a glass or ceramic dish large enough to fit all the chiles. Continue to cook the chiles for another 2–3 minutes, turning occasionally, until they are lightly browned all over, have softened and their skin has wrinkled. Remove from the pan and let stand until cool enough to handle. Carefully remove the skin, leaving the stems attached.
2. Place the cooled chiles in the dish with the garlic and sprinkle with the salt, chili flakes and bay leaves. Pour in the red wine vinegar and extra virgin olive oil, cover and cool for about 30 minutes, or until the chiles are at room temperature.
3. Place the dish in the refrigerator and chill for 2 days before serving. Remove from the refrigerator at least 30 minutes before serving.

NUTRITION PER SERVE
*Protein 2 g; Fat 20 g;
Carbohydrate 4.5 g; Dietary
Fiber 1.5 g; Cholesterol
0 mg; 200 calories*

Note: These chiles are usually eaten with either a plain tostada or fresh bread.

---

*Gambas al pil pil (top) and
Banana chiles with garlic*

Pull the tentacles away from the hood, removing the intestines at the same time.

Remove the intestines from the tentacles by cutting under the eyes.

Barbecued squid

Preparation time:
  40 minutes +
  30 minutes refrigeration
Total cooking time:
  15 minutes
Serves 6

1 lb small squid
  (calamari), (see Note)
1/4 teaspoon salt

Picada dressing
2 tablespoons extra
  virgin olive oil
2 tablespoons finely
  chopped fresh flat-leaf
  parsley
1 clove garlic, crushed
1/4 teaspoon pepper

1. To clean the squid, gently pull the tentacles away from the hood (the intestines should come away at the same time). Remove the intestines from the tentacles by cutting under the eyes, then remove the beak if it remains in the center of the tentacles by using your fingers to push up the center. Pull away the soft bone from the hood.

2. Rub the hoods under cold running water and the skin should come away easily. Wash the hoods and tentacles and drain well. Place in a bowl, add the salt and mix well. Cover and refrigerate for about 30 minutes.

3. Heat a lightly oiled barbecue griddle or preheat a broiler to its highest setting.

4. To make the picada dressing, whisk together the olive oil, parsley, garlic, pepper and some salt in a small bowl.

5. Cook the squid hoods in small batches on the barbecue griddle or under the broiler for about 2–3 minutes, or until the hoods turn white and are tender. Barbecue or broil the squid tentacles, turning to brown them all over, for 1 minute, or until they curl up. Serve hot, drizzled with the picada dressing.

NUTRITION PER SERVE
Protein 15 g; Fat 7.5 g; Carbohydrate 0.5 g; Dietary Fiber 0.5 g; Cholesterol 165 mg; 125 calories

Note: Bottleneck squid is the name given to the small variety of squid used in this recipe. If they are unavailable, choose the smallest squid you can find. This recipe is equally delicious made with cuttlefish, octopus, shrimp or even chunks of firm white fish fillet instead of the squid. Make the picada dressing as close to serving time as possible so that the parsley doesn't discolor.

Barbecued squid

Remove the beak if it remains in the center of the tentacles.

Pull the soft bone away from the hood, then rinse the hoods to remove the skin.

Artichokes in aromatic vinaigrette

Preparation time:
  15 minutes +
  2 days marinating
Total cooking time:
  None
Serves 8

1/4 teaspoon ground
  cumin
pinch ground cloves
small pinch saffron
  threads
1 clove garlic, crushed
1/3 cup white wine
  vinegar
10 oz artichoke hearts
  in oil, drained
1/3 cup extra virgin
  olive oil

1. Place the cumin, cloves, saffron, garlic, salt, pepper and a little vinegar in a mortar and pestle or small blender and pound or process to form a paste.
2. Place the artichokes in a 2 cup nonreactive dish and press down to form a tight fit.
3. Combine the paste with the remaining vinegar and oil and pour over. Cover and refrigerate for 2 days. Remove 30 minutes before serving.

NUTRITION PER SERVE
*Protein 1 g; Fat 9.5 g;
Carbohydrate 0.5 g; Dietary
Fiber 0 g; Cholesterol
0 mg; 95 calories*

Saffron and pistachio loaf

Preparation time:
  30 minutes +
  10 minutes soaking +
  1 hour 45 minutes
  proving
Total cooking time:
  20 minutes
Makes 1 loaf

2 pinches saffron
  threads
3 tablespoons hot
  water
4 teaspoons or 1 1/2 x
  1/4 oz envelopes active
  dry yeast
1 teaspoon sugar
1 cup warm water
3 cups all-purpose
  flour
2 teaspoons salt
1/2 cup pistachio nuts,
  coarsely chopped

1. Place the saffron threads and hot water in a bowl and let stand for 10 minutes. Place the yeast, sugar and warm water in another bowl. Cover and let stand in a warm place for 10 minutes, or until the mixture is foamy.
2. Mix the flour, salt and pistachios in a large bowl. Make a well in the center and add the yeast mixture and the saffron mixture (threads and all). Mix to a soft dough and gather into a ball. Turn out onto a floured surface and knead for about 5 minutes, or until the dough is elastic. Place in an oiled bowl, cover loosely with greased plastic wrap and let stand in a warm place for 1 1/4–1 1/2 hours, or until the dough has doubled in size.
3. Punch down the dough, turn out onto a floured surface and knead for 30 seconds, or until smooth. Shape into a 12 x 7 x 1/2 inch loaf. Place on a baking sheet and allow to proof in a warm place for 15 minutes. Preheat the oven to 400°F.
4. Bake for 20 minutes. To test the bread, turn upside down and tap with your fingertips. A hollow sound will tell you the bread is ready.
5. Serve the loaf warm or cold with olive oil or dips.

NUTRITION PER SLICE
*Protein 2 g; Fat 1.4 g;
Carbohydrate 9.5g; Dietary
Fiber 8 g; Cholesterol
0 mg; 59 calories*

Note: For a variation, divide the dough in half with the same measurements.

---

*Artichokes in aromatic vinaigrette (top) with
Saffron and pistachio loaf*

Garlic chicken

Preparation time:
  20 minutes
Total cooking time:
  35 minutes
Serves 6

2 lb skinless, boned
  chicken thighs
1 tablespoon paprika
2 tablespoons olive oil
8 cloves garlic,
  unpeeled
1/4 cup brandy
1/2 cup chicken stock
1 bay leaf
2 tablespoons chopped
  fresh flat-leaf parsley

1. Trim any excess fat
from the chicken and
cut the thighs into thirds.
2. Combine the paprika
with some salt and
pepper in a bowl.
Toss the chicken in the
spices. Heat half the
oil in a large skillet
over high heat and
cook the garlic for
1–2 minutes, or until
brown. Remove from
the pan and set aside.
Add half the chicken
and cook for 5 minutes,
or until brown, remove
from the pan and repeat
with the remaining
chicken, adding the
remaining oil if needed.
3. Return all the
chicken to the pan, add
the brandy, boil for

*Garlic chicken (top) with
Traditional Spanish tortilla*

30 seconds, then add
the stock and bay leaf.
Reduce the heat, cover
and simmer over low
heat for 10 minutes.
4. Meanwhile, place
the garlic pulp in a
mortar and pestle or
small bowl. Add the
parsley and pound or
mix with a fork to
make a paste. Stir into
the chicken, cover and
cook for 10 minutes, or
until tender. Serve hot.

NUTRITION PER SERVE
*Protein 40 g; Fat 10 g;
Carbohydrate 0.5 g; Dietary
Fiber 1 g; Cholesterol
85 mg; 270 calories*

Traditional
Spanish tortilla

Preparation time:
  20 minutes
Total cooking time:
  30 minutes
Serves 6–8

1/2 cup olive oil
1 lb 4 oz potatoes, cut
  into 1/4 inch slices
2 large onions,
  sliced
3 eggs
1/2 teaspoon salt
1/2 teaspoon pepper

1. Heat the oil in an
8 x 2 inch deep non-
stick skillet. Place
alternate layers of

potatoes and onions in
the pan, cover and
cook over low heat for
8 minutes. Using tongs,
turn the layers in
sections (it doesn't
matter if it all breaks
up). Cover and cook
for another 8 minutes,
without allowing the
potatoes to color.
2. Place a large strainer
over a bowl and drain
the potato mixture,
reserving 1 tablespoon
of the oil. (The rest
can be used for cooking
another time—it will
have a delicately sweet
onion flavor.)
3. Place the eggs, salt
and pepper in a bowl
and whisk to combine.
Add the potato mixture,
pressing down with
the back of a spoon to
completely cover with
the egg.
4. Heat the reserved oil
in the same skillet over
high heat. Pour in the
egg mixture, pressing
down to make an even
layer. Reduce the heat
to low, cover with a lid
or foil and cook for
12 minutes, or until
set. Gently shake the
pan to make sure the
tortilla is not sticking.
Let stand for 5 minutes,
then invert onto a
serving plate. Cut into
wedges. Serve hot.

NUTRITION PER SERVE (8)
*Protein 4.5 g; Fat 15 g;
Carbohydrate 12 g; Dietary
Fiber 1.5 g; Cholesterol
68 mg; 215 calories*

Piquant potato salad

Preparation time:
  15 minutes
Total cooking time:
  10 minutes
Serves 4

1 lb baby new potatoes
2 teaspoons chopped
  fresh dill weed
2 green onions, chopped
1 tablespoon capers,
  coarsely chopped
2 tablespoons extra
  virgin olive oil
1 1/2 tablespoons lemon
  juice
1 teaspoon finely
  grated orange rind

1. Place the baby
potatoes in a large
saucepan of water
and bring to a boil.
Cook for 10 minutes,
or until tender when
pierced with a knife.
Drain well.
2. Place the potatoes
in a bowl with the dill
weed, green onions,
capers and some salt
and pepper. Mix well
to combine. Whisk
together the oil, lemon
juice and orange rind
and pour over the hot
potatoes. Mix together
and serve warm.

NUTRITION PER SERVE
Protein 3 g; Fat 9.5 g;
Carbohydrate 15 g; Dietary
Fiber 2 g; Cholesterol
0 mg; 170 calories

Shrimp salad

Preparation time:
  30 minutes + 1 hour
  refrigeration
Total cooking time:
  None
Serves 6

1 lb 8 oz medium
  cooked shrimp,
  shelled and deveined
1 tablespoon capers,
  coarsely chopped
1 tablespoon coarsely
  chopped fresh flat-leaf
  parsley
1 green onion,
  chopped
1 tablespoon red wine
  vinegar
1 tablespoon extra
  virgin olive oil

1. Combine the shrimp,
capers, parsley, green
onion and some salt
and pepper in a
nonreactive bowl.
2. Whisk together the
red wine vinegar and
olive oil until well
blended, then pour over
the shrimp mixture and
mix well. Cover with
plastic wrap and
refrigerate for at least
1 hour, or up to 3 hours,
then serve chilled.

NUTRITION PER SERVE
Protein 25 g; Fat 4 g;
Carbohydrate 0 g; Dietary
Fiber 0 g; Cholesterol
175 mg; 135 calories

Broiled oysters

Preparation time:
  5 minutes
Total cooking time:
  5 minutes
Serves 3–4

12 oysters on the half
  shell
1/3 cup dry bread
  crumbs
1 small clove garlic,
  crushed
2 teaspoons chopped
  fresh flat-leaf parsley
2 tablespoons extra
  virgin olive oil
lemon wedges, for
  serving

1. Preheat the broiler to
medium. Remove any
grit from the surface of
the oyster flesh, then
place the oysters on a
baking sheet. Combine
the bread crumbs,
garlic, parsley and oil
in a small bowl. Season
with salt and pepper.
2. Sprinkle the crumb
mixture evenly over the
top of the oysters.
3. Broil until the
crumbs are golden,
taking care not to
overcook. Serve with
lemon wedges.

NUTRITION PER SERVE (4)
Protein 3 g; Fat 10 g;
Carbohydrate 6 g; Dietary
Fiber 1 g; Cholesterol
10 mg; 125 calories

Piquant potato salad (top) with Shrimp salad
(bottom left) and Broiled oysters (right)

Scrub the mussels well in cold water, then pull off their beards.

Remove the mussels from their shells and finely chop.

Stuffed mussels

Preparation time:
  40 minutes
  + cooling
Total cooking time:
  20 minutes
Makes 18

18 blue (common)
  mussels
2 teaspoons olive oil
2 green onions, finely
  chopped
1 clove garlic, crushed
1/4 cup chopped fresh
  flat-leaf parsley
1 tablespoon tomato
  paste
2 teaspoons lemon juice
1/3 cup dry bread
  crumbs
2 eggs, beaten
oil, for deep-frying

White sauce
3 tablespoons butter
1/4 cup all-purpose
  flour
1/3 cup milk

1. Scrub the mussels and remove their beards. Discard any open ones that do not close when given a sharp tap. Bring 1 cup water to a boil in a large saucepan, add the mussels, cover and cook for 5 minutes, shaking occasionally. Strain the liquid and measure 1/3 cup. Discard any unopened mussels. Remove the mussels from their shells and discard one half shell. Finely chop the mussels.
2. Heat the oil in a skillet, add the green onions and cook for 1 minute. Add the garlic and cook for 1 minute. Stir in the mussels, 2 tablespoons of the parsley, tomato paste, lemon juice, salt and pepper and cool.
3. To make the white sauce, heat the butter in a saucepan, add the flour and stir for

1 minute, or until just starting to color. Remove from the heat and gradually whisk in the mussel liquid, milk and some pepper. Return to the heat and boil, stirring, for 1 minute, or until the sauce is thick and leaves the side of the pan. Cool.
4. Spoon the mussel mixture into the shells. Top with the sauce and smooth so it is heaped.
5. Combine the crumbs and remaining parsley. Dip the mussels in the egg, then press in the crumbs to cover the top.
6. Fill a deep, heavy-based saucepan a third full of oil and heat to 350°F (a cube of bread dropped in the oil will brown in 15 seconds). Deep-fry in batches for 2 minutes. Drain. Serve hot.

NUTRITION PER MUSSEL
*Protein 1.5 g; Fat 7 g;
Carbohydrate 3 g; Dietary
Fiber 0.5 g; Cholesterol
30 mg; 153 calories*

Stuffed mussels

Stir the mixture until it is thick and leaves the sides of the pan.

Spoon the mussel mixture into the shells, then top with the thick white sauce.

33

Spinach, leek and pine nut rolls

Preparation time:
40 minutes + 1 hour
refrigeration
Total cooking time:
50 minutes
Serves 6–8

Pastry
1 cup all-purpose
flour
1/2 cup whole wheat
flour
1/4 teaspoon salt
1/4 cup olive oil

Filling
1 lb young spinach
1/3 cup pine nuts
1 tablespoon olive
oil
1 clove garlic,
chopped
2 leeks, white part only,
halved lengthwise and
chopped
pinch ground
cinnamon
1/3 cup dry bread
crumbs
2 eggs, lightly beaten

1. To make the pastry, sift the flours and salt into a bowl, then return the husks to the bowl. Pour in the olive oil and rub in by lifting the flour onto one hand and lightly rubbing the other hand over the top. The mixture should start to clump together.
2. Make a well in the center and add 3–4 tablespoons water, mix by hand, then add enough water to form a firm supple dough that leaves the side of the bowl. Knead gently to bring together (it may not be completely smooth). Cover with plastic wrap and refrigerate for 1 hour.
3. To make the filling, trim the stems from the spinach and discard. Wash and shred the leaves. Heat a large skillet over medium heat. Add the pine nuts and cook, stirring, for 2–3 minutes, or until lightly browned. Remove from the pan.
4. Heat the oil in the pan, add the garlic and leeks and cook, stirring occasionally, over low heat for 10 minutes, or until golden brown and caramelized. Add the spinach and stir over high heat for 3–4 minutes, or until wilted and there is no liquid left in the pan. Transfer to a bowl to cool. Stir in the pine nuts, cinnamon, bread crumbs, almost all the beaten eggs (reserving about 2 teaspoons for glazing) and salt and black pepper to taste.
5. Preheat the oven to 425°F. Lightly grease a baking sheet. Divide the dough into two portions and roll out one portion to a 10 1/2 x 8 inch rectangle. Spoon half the filling lengthwise along one half of the pastry, leaving a 3/4 inch border. Fold the other half over to shape a long roll, then fold the edges over and crimp to seal. Place on the baking sheet and repeat with the remaining pastry and filling. Brush the rolls with the reserved egg and mark with the back of a knife into six portions, taking care not to cut through the pastry. Make two small slits somewhere on the markings, through the first layer of pastry, to allow steam to escape.
6. Bake the rolls in the center of the oven for 30 minutes, or until browned and risen slightly. Allow to cool for 10 minutes before cutting through the markings into portions. Serve hot or at room temperature.

NUTRITION PER SERVE (8)
Protein 7.5 g; Fat 15 g; Carbohydrate 20 g; Dietary Fiber 4.5 g; Cholesterol 45 mg; 250 calories

Note: Delicious eaten cold on a picnic. Make individual rolls using rounds of pastry.

Spinach, leek and pine nut rolls

Banderillos

Adelicious part of the tapas table, banderillos are supposed to resemble the decorative daggers used by bullfighters with the same name. Serve on their own or with the picada or garlic dressing.

SHRIMP, EGG AND ASPARAGUS BANDERILLO

Snap the ends off 2 spears of asparagus and cut diagonally into 1 1/4 inch lengths. Cook in a saucepan of boiling water for 1 minute, drain and dry on paper towels. Shell and devein 8 small cooked shrimp. Halve 4 hard-cooked quail eggs. Thread a shrimp, half a quail egg and asparagus onto each cocktail pick. Makes 8.

OLIVE, ONION AND PIMIENTO BANDERILLO

Halve 4 stuffed green olives and 4 anchovies. Cut 1 small canned pimiento into 8 pieces. Cut a dill pickle into 8 pieces and a pickled onion into 8 wedges. Thread an olive half, a rolled up piece of pimiento, a piece of pickle and onion, a rolled up anchovy and a caper onto each cocktail pick. Makes 8.

TUNA AND PIMIENTO BANDERILLO

Halve 4 stuffed green olives. Cut 1 small canned pimiento into 8 pieces. Take 2 oz cooked fresh tuna and cut into 8 pieces. Cut a dill pickle into 8 slices. Thread a piece of olive, a piece of pimiento, a piece of tuna and pickle onto each cocktail pick. Makes 8.

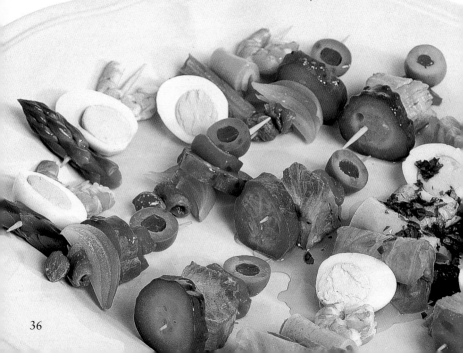

SHRIMP AND HAM BANDERILLO

Shell and devein 8 small cooked shrimp. Cut 1 oz double-smoked ham into 8 pieces, tear a lettuce leaf into 8 and halve 4 hard-cooked quail eggs. Thread a shrimp, a piece of ham, a folded up piece of lettuce and a quail egg onto each cocktail pick. Makes 8.

OLIVE, EGG AND TUNA BANDERILLO

Halve 4 stuffed green olives and 4 hard-cooked quail eggs. Cut 2 oz cooked fresh tuna into 8 pieces. Cut a small canned pimiento into 8 pieces. Thread a piece of olive, egg, tuna and a rolled up piece of pimiento onto each cocktail pick. Makes 8.

OLIVE, EGG AND ANCHOVY BANDERILLO

Have ready 8 cured black olives. Halve 4 anchovies and 4 hard-cooked quail eggs. Thread an olive, then a rolled up piece of anchovy and egg onto each cocktail pick. Makes 8.

PICADA DRESSING

Combine 2 tablespoons each extra virgin olive oil and finely chopped fresh flat-leaf parsley, 1 crushed clove garlic and some salt and pepper in a small bowl. Serve drizzled over the banderillos.

GARLIC MAYONNAISE

Place an egg in a blender with a pinch of cayenne pepper and a tablespoon of white wine vinegar. Blend until pale. Add 2 crushed cloves garlic and 1/2 teaspoon salt and combine, then pour in 3/4 cup olive oil in a thin stream with the blender on until all the oil has been added and the mixture is pale and creamy. Serve with the banderillos.

From left to right: Shrimp, egg and asparagus; Olive, onion and pimiento; Tuna and pimiento; Shrimp and ham; Olive, egg and tuna; Olive, egg and anchovy; Garlic mayonnaise

Barbecued shrimp with romesco sauce

Preparation time:
  30 minutes +
  30 minutes refrigeration
  + 15 minutes cooling
Total cooking time:
  25 minutes
Serves 6–8

30 raw large shrimp
1/4 teaspoon salt

Romesco sauce
4 cloves garlic,
  unpeeled
1 plum tomato, halved
  and seeded
2 fresh long red chiles
1/4 cup blanched
  almonds
1/3 cup sun-dried sweet
  bell peppers in oil
1 tablespoon olive oil
1 tablespoon red wine
  vinegar

1. Shell and devein the shrimp, leaving the tails intact. Mix with the salt and refrigerate for 30 minutes.
2. To make the romesco sauce, preheat the oven to 400°F. Wrap the garlic in foil and place on a baking sheet with the tomato and chiles and bake for 12 minutes. Add the almonds and bake for another 8 minutes. Cool for 15 minutes.

3. Place the almonds in a small blender or processor and blend until finely ground. Squeeze the garlic and scrape the tomato flesh into the blender, discarding the skins. Split the chiles and scrape out the seeds. Scrape the flesh into the blender, discarding the skins. Pat the sweet peppers dry with paper towels, chop and add to the blender with the oil, vinegar, some salt and 2 tablespoons water. Blend until smooth, adding more water if necessary to make a soft dipping consistency. Preheat a broiler or lightly oiled barbecue.
4. Brush the shrimp with a little oil and place on a broiler pan or straight on the barbecue. Broil or barbecue for 3 minutes, or until curled up and pink. Serve with the sauce.

NUTRITION PER SERVE (8)
Protein 45 g; Fat 8.5 g; Carbohydrate 1 g; Dietary Fiber 0.5 g; Cholesterol 315 mg; 260 calories

Note: Romesco sauce is a classic Spanish sauce traditionally served with seafood. Make up to 5 days ahead and store in the refrigerator.

Stuffed tomatoes

Preparation time:
  12 minutes
Total cooking time:
  None
Makes 8

8 small ripe tomatoes,
  about 2 inches wide
1 large ripe avocado
1 tablespoon lemon
  juice
1 small clove garlic,
  crushed
6 canned anchovy
  fillets, finely chopped
8 Spanish black olives,
  pitted and chopped
1 tablespoon snipped
  fresh chives

1. Cut a 1/2 inch slice from the base of each tomato and scoop out the seeds and membrane. Place the tomatoes, cut-side-down, on a double layer of paper towels and drain.
2. Peel and lightly mash the avocado in a small bowl. Add the lemon juice, garlic, anchovies and olives. Season to taste with salt and freshly ground black pepper.
3. Spoon the avocado mixture into the tomatoes and sprinkle with the chives.

NUTRITION PER TOMATO
Protein 2 g; Fat 7.5 g; Carbohydrate 2 g; Dietary Fiber 2 g; Cholesterol 2 mg; 85 calories

Barbecued shrimp with romesco sauce (top) with Stuffed tomatoes

Meatballs in spicy tomato sauce

Preparation time:
  40 minutes +
  30 minutes refrigeration
Total cooking time:
  30 minutes
Serves 6

6 oz lean ground pork
6 oz lean ground veal
3 cloves garlic,
  crushed
1 teaspoon ground
  coriander
1 teaspoon ground
  nutmeg
1 teaspoon ground
  cumin
pinch ground
  cinnamon
1/3 cup dry bread
  crumbs
1 egg
2 tablespoons olive
  oil

Spicy tomato sauce
1 tablespoon olive oil
1 onion, chopped
2 cloves garlic,
  crushed
1/2 cup dry white wine
16 oz can crushed
  tomatoes
1 tablespoon tomato
  paste
1/2 cup chicken stock
1/2 teaspoon cayenne
  pepper
1/2 cup frozen peas

1. Combine the pork, veal, garlic, spices, bread crumbs, egg and some salt and pepper in a bowl. Mix by hand until fairly smooth and leaving the side of the bowl. Refrigerate, covered, for 30 minutes.
2. Roll tablespoons of the mixture into balls. Heat 1 tablespoon of the olive oil in a skillet and toss half the meatballs over medium-high heat for 2–3 minutes, or until browned. Drain on paper towels. Add the remaining oil if necessary and brown the rest of the meatballs. Drain on paper towels.
3. To make the spicy tomato sauce, heat the oil in a saucepan over medium heat and add the onion. Cook, stirring occasionally, for 3 minutes, or until transparent. Add the garlic and cook for 1 minute. Increase the heat to high, add the wine and allow to boil for 1 minute. Add the tomatoes, tomato paste and stock and simmer for 10 minutes. Add the cayenne pepper, peas and meatballs. Simmer for 5–10 minutes, or until thick and the meatballs are coated in sauce. Serve hot.

NUTRITION PER SERVE
Protein 15 g; Fat 8 g; Carbohydrate 2.9 g; Dietary Fiber 0.5 g; Cholesterol 67 mg; 145 calories

Chorizo in cider

Preparation time:
  5 minutes
Total cooking time:
  15 minutes
Serves 4

1 tablespoon olive
  oil
1 small onion, finely
  chopped
1 1/2 teaspoons paprika
1/2 cup hard apple cider
1/4 cup chicken stock
1 bay leaf
8 oz chorizo sausage,
  cut into diagonal slices
2 teaspoons sherry
  vinegar, or to taste
2 teaspoons chopped
  fresh parsley

1. Heat the oil in a saucepan and fry the onion for 3 minutes, or until soft. Add the paprika and cook for 1 minute.
2. Add the cider, stock and bay leaf and bring to a boil. Reduce the heat and simmer for 5 minutes. Add the chorizo and simmer for 5 minutes to reduce the sauce slightly. Stir in the vinegar and parsley. Serve hot.

NUTRITION PER SERVE
Protein 8.5 g; Fat 20 g; Carbohydrate 4 g; Dietary Fiber 2.5 g; Cholesterol 35 mg; 255 calories

Meatballs in spicy tomato sauce (top) with Chorizo in cider

Orange and radish salad

Preparation time:
  15 minutes
Total cooking time:
  None
Serves 4

Dressing
2 tablespoons extra
  virgin olive oil
2 teaspoons lemon juice
1 teaspoon orange juice
1/4 teaspoon ground
  cumin
1/4 teaspoon sugar

4 navel oranges
4 small radishes, thinly
  sliced
12 Spanish black olives,
  pitted and cut into
  strips

1. To make the
dressing, place the olive
oil, lemon juice, orange
juice, cumin and sugar
in a small bowl and
whisk to combine.
2. Cut the skins from
the oranges, removing
all the white pith.
Using a small sharp
knife, cut between the
membranes to release
the orange segments
(do this over a bowl
to catch any juices).
Arrange the orange
segments in a circle
in a shallow serving
dish and sprinkle
with the radishes. Pile
three-quarters of the
olive strips in the center
of the dish.
3. Drizzle the dressing
over the top and
sprinkle with the
remaining olive strips.
Serve cold.

NUTRITION PER SERVE
*Protein 2 g; Fat 10 g;
Carbohydrate 15 g; Dietary
Fiber 3.5 g; Cholesterol
0 mg; 160 calories*

Note: Prepare this salad
about an hour ahead
to allow the flavors
to develop.

Beef in whisky

Preparation time:
  10 minutes
Total cooking time:
  10 minutes
Serves 6

1/2 teaspoon ground
  black pepper
12 oz thin beef round
  steak for schnitzel, cut
  into 2 1/2 inch pieces
  (see Note)
1 1/2 tablespoons olive
  oil
1 small onion, sliced
  into rings
1 clove garlic, thinly
  sliced
1/2 cup whisky
1/4 cup chicken stock
1/4 cup whipping cream

1. Sprinkle the black
pepper all over the
beef pieces. Heat
1 tablespoon of the
olive oil over high
heat in a skillet. Add
the meat in batches
and brown for
20 seconds on each
side. Remove the meat
from the skillet.
2. Reheat the skillet
over medium heat,
adding the remaining
oil if necessary. Add
the sliced onion and
cook, stirring, for
1–2 minutes, or until
soft and lightly
browned. Add the
garlic and cook,
stirring, for 1 minute.
Increase the heat to
high, add the whisky
and boil for 1 minute,
or until well reduced.
Stir in the chicken
stock and whipping
cream and simmer for
another 1 minute.
Season with salt to
taste. Return the meat
and all of the juices to
the pan and stir for
30 seconds to coat in
the sauce and reheat.
Serve hot.

NUTRITION PER SERVE
*Protein 13 g; Fat 8 g;
Carbohydrate 1 g; Dietary
Fiber 0 g; Cholesterol
725 mg; 175 calories*

Note: Ask your
butcher to cut the beef
thinly, no more than
1/4 inch thick. Veal
schnitzel can be used
instead, if preferred.

*Orange and radish salad (top) with
Beef in whisky*

Marinated sardines

Preparation time:
  40 minutes +
  30 minutes cooling +
  overnight refrigeration
Total cooking time:
  20 minutes
Makes 12

12 sardines
$1/2$ teaspoon salt
$1/4$ cup all-purpose
  flour
$1/2$ cup olive oil
4 cloves garlic
$1/2$ cup red wine
  vinegar
$1/2$ cup dry white
  wine
2 bay leaves
6 black peppercorns
$1/4$ teaspoon paprika
$1/2$ teaspoon dried
  thyme

1. To clean the sardines, scrape a small knife along the body of each sardine, starting from the tail end, to remove the scales. This is best done under cold running water. Make a slit along the gut. Cut the head and pull it away from the body slowly so that the intestines come away with the head. Open the gut cavity and clean away the remaining intestines. Pat the sardines dry on paper towels.
2. Sprinkle the sardines inside and out with the salt. Place the flour in a shallow dish and toss the sardines in the flour, shaking off the excess. Heat half the oil in a skillet over medium heat and fry the sardines in batches for 2–3 minutes on each side, or until browned all over and crisp. Place the sardines in a glass or ceramic dish and fit tightly into a single layer. Wipe the skillet clean with paper towels.

3. Heat the remaining oil in the same skillet over medium heat and add the garlic. Cook for 1–2 minutes, or until lightly browned. Place the garlic in the dish with the sardines. Add the red wine vinegar, white wine, bay leaves, peppercorns, paprika and thyme to the pan and simmer over low heat for 2 minutes. Set aside to cool for about 30 minutes. Pour the reduced mixture over the sardines, cover and refrigerate overnight, turning the sardines once during this time. Remove the sardines from the refrigerator at least 30 minutes before you are ready to serve. Serve cold.

NUTRITION PER SARDINE
Protein 20 g; Fat 14 g; Carbohydrate 2 g; Dietary Fiber 0.25g; Cholesterol 90 mg; 220 calories

---

Marinated sardines

Make a slit along the gut of the sardine with a small sharp knife.

Cut the head and pull it away slowly, taking the intestines with it.

Open up the gut cavity and remove any remaining intestines.

Pour the marinade over the sardines, cover and refrigerate overnight.

Baked polenta with spicy relish

Preparation time:
  20 minutes +
  2 hours refrigeration
Total cooking time:
  1 hour 10 minutes
Makes 48

2¹/2 cups milk
²/3 cup cornmeal
2 tablespoons butter,
  diced
1 tablespoon olive
  oil
1 tablespoon cornmeal,
  extra

Spicy relish
1 tablespoon oil
2 red onions, coarsely
  chopped
9 small plum
  tomatoes, coarsely
  chopped
1 large fresh red chile,
  finely chopped
¹/4 teaspoon Mexican
  chili powder, or to
  taste
1 tablespoon soft
  brown sugar
1 tablespoon red wine
  vinegar

1. Bring the milk to a
boil in a saucepan.
Reduce the heat and
whisk in the cornmeal
in a stream until it
thickens, then stir
constantly with a
wooden spoon for
20 minutes until it
leaves the side of the pan.
2. Remove from the
heat and stir in the
butter. Season to taste.
Spoon and spread into
a greased rectangular
cake pan about 12 x
8 inches. Smooth the
polenta and refrigerate
for 2 hours, or until set.
3. To make the spicy
tomato relish, heat the
oil in a saucepan, add
the chopped onions
and cook, stirring,
over high heat, for
3 minutes. Add the
tomatoes, chile, chili
powder, sugar and
vinegar. Simmer,
stirring occasionally,
for 20 minutes, or until
thickened. Season well.
4. Preheat the oven to
400°F. Turn the polenta
out, cut into 2 inch
squares, then into
triangles. Place on a
baking sheet covered
with parchment
(silicone) paper, brush
with olive oil and
sprinkle with the extra
cornmeal. Bake for
10 minutes, or until
the polenta is golden
and has a crust. Serve
hot or warm with the
warm relish.

NUTRITION PER PIECE
*Protein 0.5 g; Fat 1.5 g;
Carbohydrate 1.5 g; Dietary
Fiber 0 g; Cholesterol
3 mg; 25 calories*

Tomato and anchovy toasts

Preparation time:
  10 minutes
Total cooking time:
  5 minutes
Serves 4

8 x ¹/2 inch thick slices
  Italian bread
2 cloves garlic, halved
4 ripe vine-ripened
  tomatoes
2 tablespoons extra
  virgin olive oil
1¹/2 oz can anchovy
  fillets, drained and
  sliced

1. Toast the bread on
both sides until golden.
While warm, rub both
sides of the toast with
the cut garlic.
2. Cut the tomatoes
into halves and rub
each side of the toast
with some of them, so
that the juice and seeds
soak well into the toast
but do not saturate it.
Chop the remaining
tomatoes and pile on
the toasts.
3. Drizzle each toast
with the oil and top
with anchovy fillets.
Sprinkle with salt and
ground black pepper
and serve immediately.

NUTRITION PER SERVE
*Protein 9 g; Fat 12 g;
Carbohydrate 30 g; Dietary
Fiber 3 g; Cholesterol
8.5 mg; 260 calories*

---

*Baked polenta with spicy relish (top) with
Tomato and anchovy toasts*

Marinated salmon fillet

Preparation time:
  40 minutes +
  overnight marinating
Total cooking time:
  25 minutes
Serves 8–10

Marinade
1/2 cup extra virgin
  olive oil
1/4 cup white wine
  vinegar
2 tablespoons chopped
  fresh flat-leaf parsley
pinch paprika

2 lb salmon fillet
1 small red sweet bell
  pepper
2 pickled onions, finely
  chopped
2 pickled sweet
  gherkins, finely
  chopped

1. To make the marinade, whisk all the ingredients with some salt and pepper in a bowl and set aside.
2. Cut the salmon in half and place in a lightly greased steamer. Fill a saucepan half full of water, bring to a boil and sit the steamer on top. Steam, covered, for 10–12 minutes, or until the salmon is tender and cooked through. The flesh should flake easily yet still be moist. Place a pancake turner between the skin and flesh of the salmon and lift the salmon so the skin comes away. Peel away any remaining skin.
3. Place the salmon in a nonreactive dish to fit tightly in a single layer. Stir the marinade, then pour it over the hot salmon. Cover and refrigerate overnight.
4. Preheat the broiler. Cut the red pepper into quarters. Broil, skin-side-up, until the skin blackens and blisters. Place in a plastic bag and allow to cool, then peel away the skin. Slice thinly.
5. Remove the salmon from the refrigerator 30 minutes before serving. Lift out of the marinade (reserving the marinade) and cut into 1 3/4 inch pieces. Place the salmon in a dish and pour the marinade over. Sprinkle with the onion and gherkins and garnish each piece with a strip of red pepper.

NUTRITION PER SERVE (10)
Protein 1 g; Fat 14 g; Carbohydrate 1.6 g; Dietary Fiber 0.5 g; Cholesterol 0 mg; 130 calories

Note: If you don't have a steamer, place a wire rack over a saucepan of boiling water and cover with foil or a lid.

Olive twists

Preparation time:
  15 minutes
Total cooking time:
  20 minutes
Makes 50

1 tablespoon capers
4 canned anchovy fillets
2 tablespoons olive paste
  (tapenade)
1 tablespoon chopped
  fresh parsley
2 teaspoons olive oil
2 sheets ready-rolled
  puff pastry, thawed

1. Preheat the oven to 400°F. Chop the capers and anchovies and combine with the olive paste, parsley and oil. Spread a sheet of pastry with half the mixture and cut into 1/2 x 10 inch strips. Repeat with the remaining mixture and pastry.
2. Hold the ends of the strips and twist four times. Cover a baking sheet with parchment paper and bake a quarter of the strips for 5 minutes, or until golden, turning once. Repeat with the remaining twists.

NUTRITION PER TWIST
Protein 2.5 g; Fat 8.5 g; Carbohydrate 10 g; Dietary Fiber 0.5 g; Cholesterol 9.5 mg; 135 calories

---

Marinated salmon fillet (top) with Olive twists

Zucchini fritters

Preparation time:
  20 minutes
Total cooking time:
  20 minutes
Makes about 40

2/3 cup all-purpose
  flour
oil, for deep-frying
5 zucchini, cut into
  1/2 inch slices
3 tablespoons extra
  virgin olive oil
4 cloves garlic, crushed
2 canned anchovy
  fillets, finely chopped
1 tablespoon sherry
  vinegar
1 tablespoon chopped
  fresh parsley

1. Season the flour with plenty of salt and freshly ground black pepper. Fill a deep, heavy-based saucepan a third full of oil and heat to 350°F (a cube of bread dropped in the oil will brown in 15 seconds).
2. Toss the zucchini in the seasoned flour, shaking off any excess flour. Carefully drop a few zucchini slices into the oil and cook until golden brown. Drain on crumpled paper towels. Repeat with the remaining floured zucchini slices.

Zucchini fritters (top) with Shrimp fritters

3. In a small saucepan, warm the extra virgin olive oil gently over low heat for a few minutes, then add the garlic and anchovies and cook for 3 minutes without browning. Remove the pan from the heat and stir in the sherry vinegar.
4. Toss the zucchini fritters in a bowl with the garlic and anchovy oil and sprinkle the parsley over the top. These fritters are delicious served hot, and can also be eaten cold the following day.

NUTRITION PER FRITTER
Protein 0.5 g; Fat 2 g; Carbohydrate 1.5 g; Dietary Fiber 0.5 g; Cholesterol 0 mg; 30 calories

Shrimp fritters

Preparation time:
  20 minutes
Total cooking time:
  10 minutes
Makes about 30

2/3 cup all-purpose
  flour
1/3 cup self-rising
  flour
2 green onions,
  chopped
2 tablespoons chopped
  fresh flat-leaf parsley
pinch cayenne
  pepper
3/4 cup club soda
4 oz small cooked
  shrimp, shelled and
  chopped
oil, for deep-frying

1. Sift the flours into a large mixing bowl. Add the green onions, parsley, cayenne pepper and some salt and mix well. Make a well in the center, add some of the club soda and, using a whisk, gradually whisk in the flour from the sides to form a batter. Add enough of the club soda to form a batter that will drop from a spoon, then whisk until the mixture is smooth. Add the chopped shrimp and mix until everything is well combined.
2. Fill a deep, heavy-based saucepan a third full of oil and heat to 350°F (a cube of bread dropped in the oil will brown in 15 seconds). Drop scant tablespoons of the batter into the oil in batches and cook for 1–2 minutes, turning, until the fritters are puffed and evenly browned all over. Drain the fritters well on crumpled paper towels. Serve hot.

NUTRITION PER FRITTER
Protein 1.5 g; Fat 1.5 g; Carbohydrate 3 g; Dietary Fiber 0 g; Cholesterol 6 mg; 30 calories

Tostadas

Tostadas are similar to Italian bruschetta and, because they are easy to pick up, they make a great snack to have with drinks. Do not put together more than an hour in advance or they may become soggy.

BASIC TOSTADA

Preheat the broiler to high or heat a lightly oiled barbecue griddle. Cut a 1 lb (12 inch) loaf of woodfired bread into 1/2 inch thick slices. Broil or barbecue until browned. Brush one side with 2 tablespoons extra virgin olive oil. Cut a ripe tomato in half and rub onto the oiled side of the bread, squeezing the tomato to extract as much liquid as possible. Serve hot. Makes about 20.

SEARED PORK AND TOMATO TOSTADA

Have ready 8 basic tostadas. Cut 5 oz pork tenderloin into thin slices. Sprinkle the slices with salt and black pepper. Heat 2 teaspoons olive oil in a skillet and cook, in batches, for 20–30 seconds on each side, or until browned. Thinly slice a tomato. Place the pork on the tostadas and top with sliced tomato, halving the slices if they are too big. Serve hot. Makes 8.

SMOKED SALMON SALAD TOSTADA

Have ready 8 basic tostadas. Cut 6 oz smoked salmon and a small canned pimiento into strips. Place in a bowl with 2 shredded romaine lettuce leaves, 1/3 cup mayonnaise, 2 teaspoons lemon juice and a pinch of black pepper. Mix until just combined, spoon onto the tostadas and serve. Makes 8.

CHEESE AND THYME TOSTADA

Have ready 8 basic tostadas. Thinly slice 2 oz of Manchego or other semi-matured sheep's milk cheese. Top each tostada with some cheese and 1/4 teaspoon dried thyme leaves. Makes 8.

BLUE CHEESE TOSTADA

Have ready 8 basic tostadas. Place 3 oz gorgonzola cheese and 1 tablespoon brandy in a bowl. Mix with a fork until creamy, then spread on the tostadas. Sprinkle with black pepper. Makes 8.

BROILED MUSHROOM TOSTADA

Have ready 8 basic tostadas and preheat the broiler. Combine 1 tablespoon each of extra virgin olive oil and finely chopped fresh flat-leaf parsley, 1 crushed clove garlic and a good pinch of salt and black pepper in a small bowl. Remove and discard the stems and quarter 10 oz button mushrooms. Place on a foil-lined baking sheet and broil for 6 minutes, turning until browned and wilted. Place on the tostadas and drizzle with dressing. Makes 8.

CHORIZO TOSTADA

Have ready 8 basic tostadas. Heat 2 teaspoons olive oil in a skillet. Cook 6 oz chorizo sausage over low heat for 20 minutes, turning until browned all over. Remove, slice thinly and place on the tostadas. Makes 8.

From left to right: Basic; Seared pork and tomato; Smoked salmon salad; Cheese and thyme; Blue cheese; Broiled mushroom; Chorizo

Marinated seafood salad

Preparation time:
40 minutes + 2 hours
refrigeration
Total cooking time:
10 minutes
Serves 6

6 oz scallops (with roe,
optional)
12 blue (common)
mussels
2 slices lemon
2 bay leaves
pinch dried thyme
12 raw shrimp, shelled
and deveined
4 cups small broccoli
florets
1 tablespoon capers
20 dry cured olives
3 green onions,
chopped
1/2 green sweet bell
pepper, diced
1/4 cup olive oil
2 tablespoons lemon
juice
1 teaspoon Dijon
mustard
1 clove garlic, crushed

1. Remove the black
vein and small white
tendon from the
scallops. Scrub the
mussels and remove
their beards. Discard
any mussels that are
open and do not close
when given a sharp tap.
2. Place the lemon,

bay leaves, thyme and
3 cups water in a
saucepan and bring to a
boil. Add the scallops
and cook for 30–60
seconds, or until they
turn opaque. Drain on
paper towels. Add the
shrimp and cook for
2–3 minutes, or until
cooked. Drain on paper
towels. Add the
mussels, cover and
cook for 5 minutes,
or until they have
opened, shaking the
pan occasionally.
Discard any unopened
mussels, and drain on
paper towels. Discard
one half shell from
each mussel. Place the
seafood in a bowl.
3. Bring some fresh
water to a boil and
cook the broccoli for
2 minutes. Drain and
add to the seafood
with the capers, olives,
green onions and
green pepper.
4. Whisk together the
oil, juice, mustard,
garlic and some salt
and freshly ground
black pepper. Pour over
the seafood and mix
together well. Cover
with plastic wrap and
refrigerate for about
2 hours before serving.

NUTRITION PER SERVE
*Protein 18 g; Fat 3.3 g;
Carbohydrate 1.6 g; Dietary
Fiber 2.5 g; Cholesterol
100 mg; 180 calories*

Eggs scrambled with asparagus and green onion

Preparation time:
15 minutes
Total cooking time:
10 minutes
Serves 6

8 oz fresh asparagus
6 eggs
1/3 cup whipping cream
1 tablespoon olive oil
4 green onions, finely
chopped

1. Trim the woody ends
from the asparagus
and cut into 1 3/4 inch
lengths. Add the
asparagus to a
saucepan of lightly
salted boiling water.
Cook for 3 minutes,
then drain.
2. Beat the eggs, cream
and some salt and
freshly ground black
pepper in a bowl. Heat
the oil over medium
heat in a skillet, add the
green onion and cook,
stirring, for 2 minutes,
or until soft. Reduce
the heat to low, add the
asparagus and pour in
the egg and cream
mixture. Cook, gently
stirring, until creamy
and just set. Serve hot.

NUTRITION PER SERVE
*Protein 7.5 g; Fat 10 g;
Carbohydrate 1.5 g; Dietary
Fiber 1 g; Cholesterol
198 mg; 130 calories*

*Marinated seafood salad (top) with
Eggs scrambled with asparagus and green onion*

Spinach with raisins and pine nuts

Preparation time:
  15 minutes
Total cooking time:
  15 minutes
Serves 6

1 lb young spinach
2 tablespoons pine nuts
1 tablespoon olive oil
1 small red onion,
  halved and sliced
1 clove garlic, thinly
  sliced
2 tablespoons golden
  raisins
pinch ground cinnamon

1. Trim and discard the spinach stems. Wash and shred the leaves.
2. Put the pine nuts in a dry skillet and stir over medium heat for 3 minutes, or until light brown. Remove from the pan.
3. Heat the oil in the pan, add the onion and cook over low heat, stirring occasionally, for 10 minutes, or until translucent. Increase the heat to medium, add the garlic and cook for 1 minute. Add the spinach with the water clinging to it, the raisins and cinnamon. Cover and cook for 2 minutes, or until the spinach wilts. Stir in the pine nuts, and season to taste.

NUTRITION PER SERVE
*Protein 3.5 g; Fat 8 g;
Carbohydrate 4.5 g; Dietary
Fiber 3 g; Cholesterol
0 mg; 105 calories*

Bacalao with red sweet peppers

Preparation time:
  35 minutes +
  10 minutes cooling
  + 12 hours soaking
Total cooking time:
  25 minutes
Serves 6

12 oz dried salt cod or
  bacalao
1 red sweet bell pepper
1 tablespoon olive oil
1 small onion, chopped
1 clove garlic, crushed
1/4 teaspoon dried chili
  flakes
1 teaspoon paprika
1/4 cup dry white wine
2 ripe tomatoes, finely
  chopped
1 tablespoon tomato
  paste
1 tablespoon chopped
  fresh flat-leaf parsley

1. Soak the cod in plenty of water for 8–12 hours, changing the water five or six times. This will remove excess saltiness. Add the cod to a saucepan of boiling water and boil for 5 minutes. Drain and let stand for 10 minutes, or until cool enough to handle. Remove the skin and flake the fish into large pieces, removing any bones. Place in a bowl.
2. Preheat the broiler. Cut the red pepper into quarters. Broil, skin-side-up, until the skin blackens and blisters. Place in a plastic bag and let cool, then peel away the skin. Slice thinly.
3. Heat the oil in a saucepan over medium heat, add the onion and cook, stirring occasionally, for 3 minutes, or until transparent. Add the garlic, chili flakes and paprika and cook for 1 minute. Increase the heat to high, add the white wine and simmer for 30 seconds. Reduce the heat, add the tomatoes and tomato paste and cook, stirring occasionally, for 5 minutes, or until thick.
4. Add the bacalao, cover and simmer for 5 minutes. Gently stir in the red pepper and parsley and taste before seasoning with salt. Serve hot.

NUTRITION PER SERVE
*Protein 20 g; Fat 6 g;
Carbohydrate 3 g; Dietary
Fiber 1.5 g; Cholesterol
255 mg; 155 calories*

---

*Spinach with raisins and pine nuts (top) and
Bacalao with red sweet peppers*

Marinated red sweet peppers

Preparation time:
20 minutes +
3 hours or overnight
marinating
Total cooking time:
5 minutes
Serves 6

3 red sweet bell peppers
3 sprigs fresh thyme
1 clove garlic, thinly
  sliced
2 teaspoons coarsely
  chopped fresh flat-leaf
  parsley
1 bay leaf
1 green onion, sliced
1 teaspoon paprika
1/4 cup extra virgin
  olive oil
2 tablespoons red wine
  vinegar

1. Preheat the broiler.
Cut the red peppers
into quarters. Broil,
skin-side-up, until the
skin blackens and
blisters. Place in a
plastic bag and let cool,
then peel away the
skin. Slice thinly.
2. Place the peppers
in a medium glass or
ceramic bowl with the
thyme, garlic, parsley,
bay leaf and green
onion. Mix well.
3. Whisk together the
paprika, oil, vinegar

and some salt and
pepper. Pour over the
peppers mixture and
mix to combine. Cover
and refrigerate for at
least 3 hours or
preferably overnight.
Remove 30 minutes
before serving.

NUTRITION PER SERVE
*Protein 1 g; Fat 9.5 g;
Carbohydrate 2.5 g; Dietary
Fiber 1 g; Cholesterol
0 mg; 100 calories*

Note: These peppers
can be made in advance
and refrigerated for up
to 3 days.

Chickpeas and chorizo

Preparation time:
15 minutes +
overnight soaking
Total cooking time:
1 hour 10 minutes
Serves 6

3/4 cup dried chickpeas
1 bay leaf
4 cloves
1 cinnamon stick
4 cups chicken stock
2 tablespoons olive oil
1 onion, finely chopped
1 clove garlic,
  crushed
pinch dried thyme
12 oz chorizo sausage,
  chopped
1 tablespoon chopped
  fresh flat-leaf parsley

1. Soak the chickpeas
in plenty of water
overnight. Drain well,
then combine with
the bay leaf, cloves,
cinnamon stick, stock
and 5 cups water in a
large saucepan. Bring
to a boil and boil over
high heat for 1 hour,
or until the chickpeas
are tender. If they
need more time, add
a little more water.
There should be just
a little liquid left in
the pan. Remove the
bay leaf, cloves and
cinnamon stick.
2. Heat the oil in a
large skillet, add the
onion and cook over
medium heat for
3 minutes, or until
translucent. Add the
garlic and thyme and
cook, stirring, for
1 minute. Increase the
heat to medium-high,
add the chorizo and
cook for 3 minutes.
3. Add the chickpeas
and their liquid to
the pan, stir well,
then stir over medium
heat until heated
through. Remove from
the heat and stir in the
parsley. Taste before
seasoning with salt and
freshly ground black
pepper. Delicious
served hot or at room
temperature.

NUTRITION PER SERVE
*Protein 12 g; Fat 18 g;
Carbohydrate 12 g; Dietary
Fiber 5.5 g; Cholesterol
30 mg; 255 calories*

---

*Marinated red sweet peppers (top) with
Chickpeas and chorizo*

Ham and mushroom croquettes

Preparation time:
35 minutes + 2 hours
cooling + 30 minutes
refrigeration
Total cooking time:
20 minutes
Makes 18

1/3 cup butter
1 small onion, finely
   chopped
1 cup finely chopped
   mushrooms
3/4 cup all-purpose
   flour
1 cup milk
3/4 cup chicken
   stock
3/4 cup finely chopped
   cooked ham
1/2 cup all-purpose
   flour, extra
2 eggs, lightly
   beaten
1/2 cup dry bread
   crumbs
oil, for deep-frying

1. Melt the butter in a saucepan over low heat and cook the onion for 5 minutes, or until translucent. Add the mushrooms and cook, stirring occasionally over low heat, for 5 minutes. Add the flour and stir over medium-low heat for 1 minute, or until the mixture is dry and crumbly and begins to change color.
2. Remove the pan from the heat and gradually add the milk, stirring constantly until smooth. Add the stock and return to the heat, stirring constantly until the mixture boils and becomes very thick. Stir in the ham and some black pepper, then transfer to a bowl to cool for about 2 hours.
3. When completely cool, roll 3 tablespoons of the mixture into croquette shapes about 2 1/2 inches long. Place the extra flour, beaten eggs and bread crumbs in three shallow bowls. Toss the croquettes in the flour, then in the eggs, allowing the excess to drip away, then toss in the bread crumbs. Place on a baking sheet and refrigerate for about 30 minutes.
4. Fill a deep, heavy-based saucepan a third full of oil and heat to 350°F (a cube of bread dropped in the oil will brown in 15 seconds). Deep-fry the croquettes, in batches, for 3 minutes, turning to cook on all sides, until browned and heated through. Drain on crumpled paper towels. Serve hot.

NUTRITION PER CROQUETTE
*Protein 4 g; Fat 8 g;
Carbohydrate 9 g; Dietary
Fiber 0.5 g; Cholesterol
40 mg; 120 calories*

Ham and mushroom croquettes

Add the stock to the mushroom mixture and stir until it becomes thick.

Roll 2 tablespoons of the mixture into croquette shapes.

Toss the croquettes in the flour, then in the beaten eggs.

When a cube of bread browns in 15 seconds, the oil is ready to use.

Broiled tuna with olive sauce

Preparation time:
  15 minutes
Total cooking time:
  5 minutes
Serves 4

3 ripe tomatoes, peeled,
  seeded and chopped
2 tablespoons capers
2 teaspoons finely
  shredded lemon rind
1 tablespoon lemon
  juice
4 green onions, finely
  chopped
1 tablespoon chopped
  fresh flat-leaf parsley
1 clove garlic, crushed
12 Spanish black olives,
  pitted
1/4 cup extra virgin
  olive oil
1 lb 4 oz tuna steak,
  cut into 3/4 inch cubes

1. In a bowl, combine
the tomatoes, capers,
lemon rind, lemon
juice, green onions,
parsley, garlic, olives
and 3 tablespoons of
the olive oil. Season
with salt and black
pepper and set aside.
2. Heat the remaining
oil in a non-stick
skillet, add the tuna in
batches and cook
over high heat for
1–2 minutes, turning

once. The tuna should
be undercooked,
otherwise it may
become dry. Place in
a shallow dish.
3. Spoon the olive
sauce over the tuna and
serve warm.

NUTRITION PER SERVE
*Protein 35 g; Fat 4.5 g;
Carbohydrate 2.5 g; Dietary
Fiber 1.5 g; Cholesterol
105 mg; 180 calories*

Stuffed mushrooms

Preparation time:
  25 minutes + 1 hour
  cooling time
Total cooking time:
  25 minutes
Makes about 28

1 lb 12 oz open
  mushrooms
3 tablespoons butter
1 small onion, finely
  chopped
3 oz lean ground
  pork
2 oz chorizo sausage,
  finely chopped
1 tablespoon tomato
  paste
2 tablespoons dry
  bread crumbs
1 tablespoon chopped
  fresh flat-leaf parsley

1. Remove the stems
from the mushrooms,
then finely chop the

stems. Set aside.
2. Melt the butter in
a skillet over low heat,
add the onion
and cook, stirring
occasionally, for
5 minutes, or until soft.
Increase the heat to
high, add the pork, and
cook for 1 minute,
stirring constantly and
breaking up any lumps.
Add the mushroom
stems and chorizo and
continue cooking for
1 minute, or until the
mixture is dry and
browned. Add the
tomato paste and
1/2 cup water. Bring to
a boil, then reduce the
heat to low and simmer
for 5 minutes, or until
thick. Stir in the bread
crumbs, then cool for
about 1 hour.
3. Preheat the oven
to 425°F. Lightly
grease a baking sheet,
then spoon about
11/2 teaspoons of the
cooled meat mixture
into each mushroom
cap, smoothing the
top with a flexible
metal spatula so that
the filling is slightly
domed. Place on the
baking sheet and
bake in the top half
of the oven for about
10 minutes. Sprinkle
with the parsley and
serve hot.

NUTRITION PER MUSHROOM
*Protein 2.5 g; Fat 2 g;
Carbohydrate 1 g; Dietary
Fiber 1 g; Cholesterol
6.5 mg; 30 calories*

*Broiled tuna with olive sauce (top)
and Stuffed mushrooms*

Index